P9-AQA-311

No Longer Property of
Phillips Memorial Library

Stress and Reading Difficulties
Research, Assessment, Intervention

Lance M. Gentile
University of North Carolina at Asheville

Merna M. McMillan
Santa Barbara County
Health Care Services/Mental Health

Phillips Memorial
Library
Providence College

Published by the

International Reading Association
Newark, Delaware 19714

INTERNATIONAL READING ASSOCIATION

OFFICERS
1986-1987

President   Roselmina Indrisano, Boston University, Boston, Massachusetts

Vice President   Phylliss J. Adams, University of Denver, Denver, Colorado

Vice President Elect   Patricia S. Koppman, PSK Associates, San Diego, California

Executive Director   Ronald W. Mitchell, International Reading Association, Newark, Delaware

DIRECTORS

Term Expiring Spring 1987
> Carl Braun, University of Calgary, Calgary, Alberta, Canada
> Nora Forester, Northside Independent School District, San Antonio, Texas
> Susan Mandel Glazer, Rider College, Lawrenceville, New Jersey

Term Expiring Spring 1988
> Margaret Pope Hartley, The Psychological Corporation, North Little Rock, Arkansas
> P. David Pearson, University of Illinois, Champaign, Illinois
> Carol M. Santa, School District #5, Kalispell, Montana

Term Expiring Spring 1989
> Marie C. DiBiasio, Bristol Public Schools, Bristol, Rhode Island
> Hans U. Grundin, The Open University, Milton Keynes, England
> Nancy E. Seminoff, Winona State University, Winona, Minnesota

Copyright 1987 by the
International Reading Association, Inc.

Library of Congress Cataloging-in-Publication Data

Gentile, Lance M.
    Stress and reading difficulties.

    Bibliography: p.
    1. Reading disability. 2. Stress (Psychology)
3. Reading — Remedial teaching. I. McMillan, Merna M.
II. Title.
LB1050.5.G39   1987   428.4'2   87-2643
ISBN 0-87207-783-7

Cover by Boni Nash

Contents

IRA DIRECTOR OF PUBLICATIONS   Jennifer A. Stevenson

IRA PUBLICATIONS COMMITTEE 1986-1987   James E. Flood, San Diego State University, *Chair* • James F. Baumann, Purdue University • Janet R. Binkley, IRA •Rudine Sims Bishop, The Ohio State University • Carl Braun, University of Calgary • Susan W. Brennan, IRA • Richard L. Carner, University of Miami • Richard C. Culyer III, Coker College • Dolores Durkin, University of Illinois • Philip Gough, University of Texas at Austin • John Micklos, IRA • Ronald W. Mitchell, IRA • Joy N. Monahan, Orange County Public Schools, Orlando, Florida • Allan R. Neilsen, Mount St. Vincent University • John J. Pikulski, University of Delaware • María Elena Rodríguez, IRA, Buenos Aires • Robert Schreiner, University of Minnesota • Jennifer A. Stevenson, IRA

The International Reading Association attempts, through its publications, to provide a forum for a wide spectrum of opinions on reading. This policy permits divergent viewpoints without assuming the endorsement of the Association.

Foreword

W hen children experience difficulties in school, their problems are often compounded by a number of other factors. Constant failure and frustration may lead to strong feelings of inferiority, which, in turn, may intensify initial learning deficiencies. Under the impact of continued failure, children may withdraw or may act aggressively. Interpersonal relationships may suffer; children may displace many of their problems onto their home situation. All of this suggests the importance of children's school experiences and their ability to make efficient use of their thinking processes in ultimate adaptation to the world around them.

It is justifiable to say that most children with severe reading difficulties have emotional problems resulting from constant failure. Nevertheless, the converse is frequently true; emotional conflicts may result in reading problems. For example, children may bring so much conflict to the reading situation that they cannot be receptive even in the best of circumstances. Still other children bring so much anxiety to the learning situation that it becomes almost impossible for them to focus their attention on the teacher for more than a short period of time.

While much attention has been devoted to the improvement of educational strategies, there has not been a similar focus on the personality of the child with a reading disability. In this book, Gentile and McMillan go a long way toward rectifying this situation. Focusing on the concept of stress, their thesis is that feelings play an extremely important role in determining children's motivation for reading, their ability to use their resources for learning to read, and the degree of efficacy of the learning process. It is the authors' opinion that, in their zeal to develop more efficient instructional strategies, educators neglect the psychological significance of stress in the learning situation.

In 1936, Hans Selye first postulated the important concepts that led to the principles of the General Adaptation Syndrome. Derivatives of these significant ideas are found in almost every area of normal psychological development, as well as in psychopathology. Yet, to a very large extent, these same important principles have been relatively neglected by those in the field of education. Gentile and McMillan are aware of this neglect, and they set out to help teachers identify specific stress reactions to reading and to suggest ways to overcome the negative aspects of stress.

This book makes a major contribution to our understanding of the relationship of emotional maladjustment and reading and, perhaps more importantly, to our knowledge of what to do about it. Specific techniques are described, all designed to help the disabled reader deal with the stress of frustration or to limit the possibility of frustration. Through it all, Gentile and McMillan convincingly show that they conceptualize no dichotomy between the cognitive realm and the affective sphere. No matter what may be the primary etiological factor of the reading disability, the child's continued failure to read is sustained by an aversive reaction to reading, the impact of prolonged reading failure, and the reaction of the organism to stress. This is the authors' message, and they present it forcefully and impressively.

Jules C. Abrams
Hahnemann University

Introduction

For seventy-five years research has confirmed that students with reading difficulties have emotional disturbances and students with emotional disturbances have reading difficulties. A "chicken or egg" controversy has developed that is extremely complex and remains unresolved. It continues today unabated and has contributed to the proliferation of studies in medicine, psychology, and education that focus on identifying the problem, labeling it, and deliberating about symptoms instead of solutions. While all the questions concerning etiology may never be answered, one of the most crucial factors that has been identified is emotional adjustment in reading. Abrams (1983, p. 478) described the emotional plight of children experiencing difficulty with reading:

> There is little doubt that youngsters who have suffered with reading disability over any sustained period of time are going to have serious questions about themselves and their abilities. Constantly frustrated, beseiged with intense feelings of defectiveness, it is no wonder that they react with hostility and various forms of acting out behavior. Is it any wonder that retarded readers are emotionally less well-adjusted, less stable, insecure and fearful in relation to emotionally challenging situations? Many of these children must feel helpless in the face of their inability to read. And, when they feel this way, they become even more frightened and anxious. As a result, they tend to become either more aggressive, more hostile, or sometimes withdrawn.

Our purpose in writing this monograph is to move past the circular debate. We offer what we have learned to encourage researchers to escape the "paralysis from analysis" trap, to help teachers improve students' reading performance, and ultimately to help teachers make positive changes in the lives of those students whose reading and academic progress is unnecessarily jeopardized by disabling stress reactions.

This monograph is based on our research and teaching and that of others, our supervision of teachers in classrooms and clinics, and interviews with parents and family members. Most importantly, it is derived from many years of analyzing and reflecting on our work with hundreds of students and adults referred for reading difficulties.

There are risks in using this information to describe a theoretical framework for application in the classroom when the etiology is unknown and inferences must be made about the mediation processes of the human mind. But, if the result is better adjusted, less stressed readers who have learned effective coping skills that may generalize to other areas of their lives, then the academic risk of making some inferences and assumptions is warranted. It is time we in reading move from the debate over etiology to developing, implementing, and studying effective intervention.

In this monograph, we will consider stress as a significant factor in emotional maladjustment to reading. Toward this end, we will (1) examine some of the pertinent research related to emotional maladjustment in reading; (2) introduce an instrument to assist teachers in identifying specific stress reactions to reading; and (3) suggest effective approaches for working with students who are experiencing stress that may be either the source or result of their reading difficulties.

LMG
MMM

1
Research on emotional maladjustment in reading

> The greatest thing a human soul ever does in this world is to see
> something and tell what he saw in a plain way.
>
> John Ruskin
> *Modern Painters*

Many researchers have investigated the effects of emotions on learning to read, reading performance, and reading failure. However, their work has never been synthesized into a cohesive body of knowledge. Gentile and McMillan (1983, p. 484) argue that unless the information is organized and interpreted, "future investigators will continue to generate repetitive research that leads to more cataloguing of children's emotional and reading difficulties, but fails to provide applicable solutions."

After an extensive review of reading research in the areas of self-concept, social learning, and cognitive style, Athey (1985, p. 540) hypothesized that good readers are "relatively free from anxiety and neurotic manifestations, while poor readers...exhibit more symptoms of maladjustment, especially [in] school."

The following literature review reveals a striking coherence supporting Athey's hypothesis. It is organized to relate stress, stressors, and stress reactions to emotional maladjustment in reading. This approach provides both a framework for interpreting this body of knowledge and a theoretical basis for developing effective intervention.

Stress

There is nothing good or bad, but thinking makes it so.
William Shakespeare

Cannon (1915) described the physiological and psychological effects of stress in terms of fight or flight, claiming these reactions occur as the result of any real or perceived threat to the organism. He used the term *homeostasis* for the body's ability to adapt to stress.

Selye (1956) defined stress as the common factor in all of the body's adaptive reactions and concluded that stress is essentially the rate of wear and tear on the body. It can occur as *eustress,* which is pleasant and curative, or *distress,* which is unpleasant and disease producing. Selye used the term *general adaptation syndrome* to refer to all of the changes in the body that occur from stress. These changes affect both the structure and chemical composition of the body. Rutter (1983, p. 1) concluded that the effect of stress on the body is the same regardless of its source.

Stress is the body's response to any extra demand made upon it. Selye (1976) identified situations, events, or people who produce stress reactions as *stressors* and listed the following signs of stress: general irritability, hyperexcitation, or depression; impulsive behavior, emotional instability; inability to concentrate; nonspecific or floating anxiety; stuttering and other speech difficulties; and physical manifestations such as headaches, stomachaches, and excessive perspiration.

Selye's work helped demonstrate that stress causes the body to react physiologically according to Cannon's postulated fight or flight syndrome. When a person perceives a situation to be stressful, the body increases its production of hormones such as epinephrine and norepinephrine to prepare itself for action. These hormones increase heart rate, blood volume, and blood pressure and reduce the flow of blood to the hands and feet in order to channel it to the larger muscle groups that are critical for a quick physical response. Lloyd-Kolkin (1986, p.1) stated:

A stressful situation in which an immediate response is not possible may produce an ongoing feeling of anxiety or helplessness in the individual, since the body under chronic stress produces large amounts of corticosteroids which increase the heart rate and the volume of blood the heart pumps per second. The individual under prolonged stress experiences a feeling of hypervigilance, muscle tension, and considerable unease.

Gentile and McMillan

Research results on emotional maladjustment and reading difficulties indicate many students perceive reading as threatening and respond to it according to Cannon's fight or flight syndrome.

The association of stress and reading difficulties is buttressed by a wide body of research and learning theory. These studies and theories are reviewed under the headings of Stressors in reading and Stress reactions to reading.

Stressors in reading

Fear is an expectation of evil. Under fear are arranged the following emotions: terror, nervous shrinking, shame, consternation, panic, mental agony. Terror is fear which produces fright; shame is fear of disgrace; nervous shrinking is a fear that one will have to act; consternation is fear due to a presentation of some unusual occurrence; panic is fear with pressure exercised by sound; mental agony is fear felt when some issue is still in suspense.

Zeno the Stoic
Quoted in Diogenes Laërtius, "Zeno"

Many children who experience difficulties learning to read are punished and made to feel inferior or inadequate for their reading problems (Wilson, 1981). They are frequently subjected to embarrassment and criticism from parents, teachers, and peers. Moreover, they are made to read aloud and are interrupted frequently to correct their reading errors (Allington, 1980). Gradually, many of these youngsters develop feelings ranging from anger to apprehension because they sense they have no control over what happens to them during reading. Such children also can feel trapped and see themselves contending with oppressive, nonsupportive supervison. In their perception, it is unlikely they will ever be good enough readers to satisify the demands or expectations of parents, teachers, and peers. To make matters worse, many of these youngsters feel guilty and are emotionally upset or stressed because they think they have let their parents or teachers down. They are often unable to express their inner feelings for fear of reprisal.

Gentile and McMillan (1984, p. 9) summarized these problems: Many youngsters feel threatened by the demands some teachers make during reading instruction. The teachers' practices are not necessarily stressful when used with successful readers, but when they are used with students who experience difficulty reading they can create serious emotional conflicts. These threatening practices include the following:

- Requiring students to read aloud in front of other children. During oral reading teachers frequently interrupt students to correct their pronunciation, tempo, rate, and lack of appropriate inflection or expression.
- Requiring students to stand up before the class and act out parts of stories or plays that require reading difficult lines or passages in front of their peers.
- Requiring students to read from books or materials that are either too long or too hard for them and then having them reread when this serves no constructive purpose.
- Requiring students to read aloud from material that is obviously more appropriate for younger children.
- Requiring students to stop reading because they have made too many errors or appear lost or confused. At this point teachers often ask some other student to "help" the youngster locate certain pieces of information, find the right place in the book or material, pronounce certain words, answer questions, or make more accurate interpretations.
- Requiring students to read and then, in a misguided attempt at humor, mimicking or commenting upon the quality of the student's reading or behavior.
- Requiring students to do the same kind of reading day after day from basal readers and to complete innumerable workbook activities in order to overcome skills deficits. These activities frequently bore students, and boredom or lack of purpose is stressful and frustrating. The attempt to strengthen weaknesses by focusing solely on them does nothing to alter students' perceptions of themselves as poor readers. In fact, quite the opposite may be true. By constantly having to face or confront these weaknesses, students' perceived incompetencies actually may be confirmed.
- Requiring students to read material that parallels specific traumatic conditions in their lives. Bibliotherapy is appropriate in some circumstances, but should be used with sensitivity so as not to contribute to a student's anxiety or feelings of inadequacy.

Lynch et al. (1981) found that blood pressure rises significantly when an individual starts talking. When a person speaks to strangers, argues, or is criticized, the level of stress that occurs can be measured by blood pressure elevation as great as 40 to 50 percent above resting levels observed in the laboratory. These findings have significance for many children who experience stress in school while trying to adjust to an environment different from their own homes, who encounter criticism and rebuke for their errors in reading, and whose failure to develop "normal" reading skills is a constant source of frustration or embarrassment.

Furthermore, what many school children feel in such situations may be intensified because of what Kagan (1983, p. 192) has described as a major principle vital to any discussion of stress, that the "consequences of an event are dependent upon structural readiness of the organism." Gentile and Lamb (1984) measured primary school children's developmental readiness or maturity for reading. Among the twelve subjects tested, using the Gesell Developmental Examination, five scored six months or more below their chronological ages; three of these showed discrepancies of more than one full year. While the small number of children in this study limits generalizations, it may be that lack of readiness or maturity for reading is a factor in some school children's reading difficulties. More important, being required to learn to read before reaching an appropriate developmental age may create additional stress for children. This area needs to be studied more rigorously using statistically reliable methods. To date, most of the assessment practices related to developmental age in reading lean heavily on subjective interpretations to determine a child's level of readiness.

Other research points to the broader effects of stress in reading. Deci (1985) indicated teachers are under excessive pressure to increase students' standardized reading achievement test scores. A study by Deci et al. (1982) showed that stress produced by this pressure makes teachers more controlling than they know they should be. The additional mandates of professional performance standards and achievement standards for their students make the pressures even stronger and elicit even more rigidity and control.

Elkind (1981) observed a rising state of depression among many school children. In their study of children whose parents had been recently divorced, Kelly and Wallerstein (1976) found both physiological and psychological problems that arise from depression among school aged children. Weinberg and Rehmet (1983) confirmed a high rate of depression in children referred for reading and learning difficulties. These researchers' concern for the lack of proper diagnosis led them to develop a scale by which a child's depressive tendencies can be measured.

When school children are depressed, it may interfere with their capacities for reading. The fact they experience difficulty or failure in reading may then add to negative feelings of self-worth and increase their rate of depression (Lamb, 1985). Moreover, depression can be manifested in passive or aggressive ways in children and adolescents and is often overlooked or underdiagnosed when characterized by acting out behavior.

Stress reactions to reading

...for the hardest victory is the victory over self.

Aristotle
Quoted in Stobaeus, *Floritegium*

Spache (1976) cited 64 studies that relate emotional maladjustment and reading difficulties to depression, aggresion, resentment, resistance, hostility, anxiety, withdrawal, impulsiveness, rigidity, defensiveness, and other acting out behaviors. According to Cannon and Selye's research, these behaviors can be considered fight or flight stress reactions to reading when reading is perceived to be threatening.

Lecky (1951, p. 162) described how resistance or fight reactions adversely affect learning:

> Resistance is the opposite to assimilation and learning, and represents the refusal to reorganize the values, especially the ego values....To the educator, it appears as an obstacle to learning. But if we would really understand these resistances, we must see them not as neurotic or abnormal manifestations, but as wholly natural devices for avoiding reorganization.

Various learning theories allude to stress reactions affecting reading performance. Freud (1935) described how young children's dependence on adults for approval can facilitate education. If the important relationships children have with parents and other adults are disruptive, hostility can result. This hostility can generalize to school and may affect reading adversely. In a later publication (1937), Freud spoke of how children use energy reserves to repress feelings that are difficult to deal with. In such cases, there might well be little energy left for academic tasks such as reading.

Skinner (1972) contends that behavior is a product of operant conditioning. Applying this theory to reading, teachers affect the probability of students' responses by the consequences they arrange. The conditions can be positive, involving approach and continuation, or negative, involving avoidance. The student's reaction is influenced by the conditions and consequences established by the teacher or others. Skinner summarized by saying that an "organism can be reinforced by—can be made to 'choose'— almost any given state of affairs" (p. 33).

Another theory postulates that operant conditioning does not adequately reflect human behavior unless an element of expectancy is added. According to this theory, rewarding a behavior strengthens the behavior indirectly by strengthening the expectancy that the behavior will produce future rewards. In human beings old enough to form concepts and have some awareness of complex causes, many factors can influence expectations of rewards, including past experience, current information, and one's estimate of the situation.

Rotter (1966) suggests that one of the most important factors contributing to this expectancy is the individual's belief in the extent to which he or she can affect the outcome of a situation. Belief varies from situation to situation, but some people believe they can control events, while others believe they are perpetually at the mercy of forces beyond their control. This latter belief is often characteristic of poor readers and, as might be expected, is frequently accompanied by anxiety (Athey, 1985).

Dreikurs, Grunwald, and Pepper (1971, p. 220) emphasized the importance of identifying the psychological factors in reading:

> Organic or physiological concepts lead to an underestimation of the psychological factors of reading difficulties. Even when cultural or social factors are taken into consideration, they prevent rather than facilitate an understanding of the child's problems. Without comprehension of his goals, the significance of his disfunctions and deficiencies cannot be determined. Corrective measures require an understanding of the child's concepts, private logic, and goals. Even if he is physically deficient or culturally deprived, it is his reaction to the conditions that explains his behavior. What a child has is less important than what he does with it.

In 1908, Huey described the mental energy and level of concentration required for reading. In the ensuing years, many researchers have identified a connection between emotional disturbances, the resulting loss of concentration, and reading difficulties (deHirsch, Jansky, & Langford, 1966; Dolch, 1931, 1951; Dreikurs and Soltz, 1964; Gentile, McMillan, and Swain, 1985; Gray, 1925; Johnson, 1985; Kagan and Havemann, 1972; Monroe, 1932; Natchez, 1959, 1968; Osborn, 1951; Robinson, 1946, 1964; Roswell and Natchez, 1977; Sherman, 1939; Young and Gaier, 1951).

Gray (1922) listed fourteen causes of reading difficulties; four point directly to stress: narrow attention span, inadequate attention to content, lack of interest, and timidity.

After working with fifteen cases of reading difficulty, Hincks (1925) reported that the children exhibited behaviors such as nightmares, hypochondria, oversensitivity, and emotional outbreaks.

Monroe (1932) compared 415 children with reading problems with other children from the same child guidance clinic. Among students with reading difficulties, she found more emotional disturbance in the form of daydreaming, temper tantrums, and enuresis.

In a study of the psychological difference between 300 advanced readers and 300 problem readers, Jackson (1944) found that fears, worries, and other emotional factors were so prevalent among problem readers that they merited special attention in addition to attention to reading difficulties.

Gann (1945) studied 100 boys and girls from grades three through six who were having reading problems, attempting to discover whether reading difficulties are aspects of the total personality. Using the Rorschach test and other instruments to measure traits such as persistence, concentration, and impulsiveness, Gann found that problem readers are emotionally less well-adjusted, less stable, and less socially adaptable than good readers. They are also insecure and fearful in emotionally challenging situations.

Bird (1927) studied why some children of the same age and intellectual capacity learn to read more easily than others. He found wide differences among these children at the beginning stages of reading. One-third of the students seemed to make steady improvement with no more conspicuous delays than might be expected from young children just entering school; one-third had occasional but unmistakable personality traits that interfered with their progress; and one-third had habits that diverted their attention from the reading task. Thus, Bird concluded that learning was blocked by emotional problems in 67 percent of the children he studied.

Family problems contributed to emotional disturbances that resulted in reading problems in 54 percent of the children studied by Robinson (1939). In follow-up studies involving 30 cases, Robinson enlisted the help of a social worker, psychiatrist, pediatrician, neurologist, speech correction specialist, otolaryngologist, endocrinologist, reading specialist, psychologist, and three ophthalmologists. These interdisciplinary professionals identified social and emotional difficulties as the most frequent causes of poor progress in reading.

According to Gates (1941), emotional patterns revealed by clinical analysis can partially explain some reading problems. After studying the research of others as well as his own case file, Gates concluded that no single personality pattern characterizes reading failure; that certain emotional or motivational patterns, revealed by clinical analysis, may partially account for many students' reading problems; and that the emotional tension, anxiety, fear, or resistance that often appears among students while they are learning to read interferes with their learning.

Gates also postulated that the more serious the reading retardation in a child, the greater the probability that the child will also have an emotional maladjustment. He estimated that 75 percent of cases marked by reading difficulties show some degree of personality maladjustment.

Blanchard (1936) showed an intimate relationship between emotional tensions and failure to perform well in reading. Believing these findings proved an existing relationship between emotional disturbances and reading problems, Missildine (1946) urged researchers to investigate the nature of the relationship, seeking recurring patterns in the emotional disturbances of children with reading disabilities. Missildine investigated thirty case histories of children who were being seen in the children's psychiatric service at The Johns Hopkins University Hospital between 1936 and 1944. Twenty of these thirty children had mothers who were aggressive, perfectionistic, or overtly hostile toward them. These mothers described their children as happy-go-lucky, irresponsible, restless, and afraid of the dark. They also said these were stubborn youngsters on whom punishment had little effect. Although professional observers found these children polite, cooperative, and friendly, they also determined them to be insecure, restless, restrained, and unhappy. Missildine concluded that reading disability is a symptom of underlying emotional illness in many children who have reading problems and who do not respond to specific remedial techniques.

Not all early studies support this view. A number of researchers saw reading problems not as the result but as the cause for emotional disturbance. In fact, Spache (1976, p. 242) claimed that few "have recognized the equally plausible deduction that the symptoms of maladjustment might have appeared because of the reading failure."

Preston (1940) studied 100 students who were failing in reading and associated the emotional effects of their reading with emotional maladjustment as children. Wiskell (1948), working with students referred to a college reading clinic, noted that years of failure in reading produced inferiority complexes, frustration, and other emotional problems.

However, Paynter and Blanchard (1929) argued there was insufficient evidence to prove that reading problems were caused by emotional disturbances. Robinson (1946, p. 78) suggested that the two problems might be interactive:

> It seems evident that emotional difficulties may cause reading disabilty in the beginning and that this disability may, in turn, result in frustration, which further blocks learning and again intensifies the frustration. The interaction and intensification become a vicious cycle, leading to intense emotional maladjustments and complete failure to progress in reading.

Others stopped short of agreeing there could be a causal relationship between emotional disturbances and reading difficulties, but saw a possible interaction of emotional factors with other variables to produce these problems. Dahlberg, Roswell, and Chall (1952, p. 211) wrote:

> Whether the emotional disturbance is the cause, effect, or a concomitant feature of the reading disability is not always clear, but that emotional disturbance characterizes most children with severe reading disabilities is a fact that remedial teachers know only too well.

Summary

Research points to a connection between stress and reading difficulties. Many studies suggest students with reading difficulties demonstrate behavior associated with emotional maladjustment in their private lives, at school, or both. When students experience emotional trauma during reading, the emotional drainage that occurs may seriously limit their willingness or ability to concentrate. Under these circumstances, reading may evoke specific maladaptive stress reactions that inhibit students' learning. These reactions have been found to be both physical and psychological and are manifested in a range of behavior from anger and aggression (fight) to avoidance and apprehension (flight). Finally, some studies show that, overtly or covertly, parents, teachers, or peers may contribute toward making reading threatening or stressful.

In the research, the issue of cause and effect in relation to reading difficulty and emotional maladjustment remains unresolved. The circular debate has done little to contribute to practical and effective intervention. Using the framework of perceived threat and fight or flight reactions to reading offers an explanation that can be used to identify both the source and solution to the problems some students have with reading. It also provides teachers with information about the role they can play in making reading less stressful for students and teaching less stressful for themselves.

2
Assessment

Appearance overpowers even the truth.

Simonides of Ceos
The Spartans of Thermopylae

Most efforts to measure and remediate reading difficulties are based on standardized or informal skills tests. Underlying these tests is the notion that if teachers can identify specific skills deficits, they will be able to find an instructional cure to relieve these symptoms of reading difficulty. This reductionist view of reading may contribute to the fact that research fails to show many long term gains or lasting effects of remedial reading instruction. Johnson (1985, pp. 174-175) noted:

> Past attempts at explanations of the differences between good and poor readers have tended to dwell on the minutiae of mental operations without considering either the psychological or social contexts in which they occur....Most current explanations of reading difficulties focus on the level of operations, devoid of context, goals, motives, or history. While some work has focused on the context of reading failure rather than mental operations (McDermott, 1977; Mehan, 1979), there has been little effort to integrate these two dimensions. The consequent explanations of reading failure are sterile and have resulted in more or less terminal diagnoses of reading failure. Until we can integrate the depth of human feeling and thinking into our understanding of reading difficulties, we will have only a shadow of an explanation of the problem and ill-directed attempts at solutions.

One major reason most remedial reading programs focus only on skills deficits is because school administrators and state legislators use only the results of standardized reading skills tests for determining good and poor readers, comparing schools, and judging teacher effectiveness. While these tests may be a useful measure for comparing students within or among groups, they should not be used as the sole basis for designing remediation in reading. According to Moffett (1985, p. 52), "If it's not tested, it's not taught."

Assessment and intervention must go beyond skills deficits and consider the following points:

- It is as important to understand, measure, and address the social and emotional variables that form the core of many students' struggles or failures in reading as it is to test and evaluate their basic reading skills deficits. Relying solely on skills deficits to identify students' difficulties in reading is inadequate for helping them learn to read and make a better adjustment to reading.
- The whole of reading is greater than the sum of the parts. Undeniably, skills are important in reading, as is time on task skills practice, but social and emotional adjustments determine how little or how much a student brings to and derives from reading and reading instruction (Dreikurs, 1954; Gentile and McMillan, 1981).
- Many students with reading difficulties can demonstrate some level of skills mastery compared to other students of the same age or grade level (Lamb, 1985), but standardized test results fail to show what students are capable of doing. In most cases, results of skills tests reveal the approximate level at which a student's growth in reading stops. Missing from these test results are three important pieces of information relevant to helping students learn to cope effectively with reading difficulty: What did students do when the test became difficult? What coping skills did they demonstrate? What influence did these coping skills have on test performance? (Gentile, McMillan, and Swain, 1985).

Students' perceptions of their reading capabilities during testing or studying affect what they choose to do, how much effort they mobilize, how long they persevere in the face of difficulties, their thought patterns, and the amount of stress they experience in taxing situations.

Successful readers respond flexibly to the emotional challenges of tests and reading assignments. They do not perceive reading as a threat; they do anticipate positive results for their efforts. Consequently, they have developed reading skills and study habits that permit them to work effectively, to assume responsibility for their own learning, to be comfortable and relaxed while reading, and to resolve their own difficulties.

In general, most successful readers are accepted by their peers. They are supported and encouraged by parents and teachers who expect them to succeed. Usually they are friendly, polite, and cooperative. They read independently, concentrate, and complete assignments satisfactorily and on time. While they may experience some difficulty or make mistakes in reading, they cope effectively and show steady improvement. They have learned to overcome problems through diligence, patience, and focused, consistent effort. They recognize their limitations, yet work to strengthen their reading. Teachers experience little if any stress in working with these students.

On the other hand, poor readers face many problems in addition to their skills deficits. They perceive reading as a threat and frequently exhibit maladaptive stress reactions when they read. These patterns of responses are significant because they have the capacity to dictate and disrupt all future experiences with written matter (Laurita, 1985). They perceive reading as a threat and frequently exhibit maladaptive stress reactions when they read. Poor readers also display self-deprecation, lack of clear goals or values, vulnerability to disparagement by others, immature relationships with parents or teachers, lack of insight into personal problems, or pervasive depression (Maxwell, 1971).

Because a skills based approach does nothing to alleviate students' perceptions of reading as threatening, working with these students is often frustrating and stressful for teachers. As a result, teachers may also manifest fight or flight reactions. This highlights the need for changes in teacher training, assessment, intervention, and program design.

Other researchers have provided detailed descriptions of students' maladaptive stress reactions to reading. Gentile and McMillan (1984) and Swain (1985) analyzed the records of 500 students with reading difficulties referred to an interdisciplinary diagnostic and remedial center. All the students were given a full multidisciplinary assessment; none was diagnosed as having neurological or other physical impairments that would alter the expectation of normal development in reading. Data were drawn from referral and evaluation statements of parents, teachers, reading specialists, and counselors; observational information recorded during the administration of formal and informal tests; and statements from diagnostic or prescriptive reports. The descriptions were then consolidated and classified. What emerged was a spectrum of fight or flight behavioral categories ranging from hostility and rage to immobilization and retreat.

Stress Reaction Scale for Reading

Besides learning to see, there is another art to be learned—not to see what is not.

Maria Mitchell
Life, Letters and Journals

From these studies Gentile and McMillan (1984) developed the Stress Reaction Scale for Reading. This scale can be used to identify students' maladaptive reactions to reading and to guide the use of appropriate instructional techniques. The instrument is designed to provide an overall impression of students' reactions to reading. Because of the complexity of reading problems, these emotional reactions are difficult to categorize precisely. Rather, the Scale is intended to show behavior trends when reading is stressful. The scale is not all inclusive and should be used only as an observational tool.

Stress Reaction Scale for Reading

For each of the following phrases, circle the letter, *a* or *b,* that most accurately describes the student's reactions when asked to read or during reading. If *neither one* applies, write *N/O* on the blank to the right of each pair.

When asked to read or during reading, this student:

1. a. exhibits hostility or rage.
   b. becomes anxious or apprehensive. _____

2. a. becomes sullen or exhibits aggressive acting out behavior.
   b. appears indifferent, insecure, or fearful. _____

3. a. responds impulsively to requests or questions, blurts out answers, and offers information that is irrelevant or inaccurate.
   b. appears subdued, overly withdrawn, and depressed. _____

4. a. throws temper tantrums, cries, or becomes verbally abusive.
   b. seeks an escape or runs and hides. _____

5. a. clenches fists, becomes rigid, defiant, and angry.
   b. appears despondent, passive, and unable to concentrate. _____

6. a. becomes defensive and resistive, verbalizes or expresses an attitude of "I don't want to."
   b. lacks confidence, appears timid, verbalizes or expresses an attitude of "I can't, it's too hard." _____

7. a. demands entertaining, easy, or expedient activities, shows no tolerance for difficulty or challenge.
   b. takes no risks in challenging situations, constantly answers "I don't know," even when answers are obvious. _____

8. a. refuses to comply, does not follow directions or complete assignments.
   b. appears embarassed, daydreams, or frets over lack of ability. _____

9. a. becomes upset with change in routine, manipulates the situation to satisfy personal needs or whims.
   b. requires constant assurance, frequently checks with teacher by asking "Did I get that right?" or "Was that good?" _____

10. a. seeks to disrupt the teacher, the lesson, or other students.
    b. expresses fear of rejection by parents, teachers, or peers for reading weaknesses. _____

11. a. uses any excuse for not being able to participate, temporizes until parent or teacher gives up.
    b. skips over material, ignores punctuation, inserts or deletes words and phrases, unable to follow structure or order. _____

12. a. demands constant supervision, attention, or guidance, refuses to do any independent reading.
    b. will try as long as parent or teacher closely monitors situation, appears helpless when left to work independently. _____

13. a. provides sarcastic, bizarre, or nonsensical answers to teachers' questions, makes weird sounds, sings, or bursts into loud, raucous laughter.
    b. becomes excessively self-critical, says things like "I'm dumb," "I never get anything right," or "I'm not a good reader." _____

14. a. declares reading is "boring," "no fun," "hard work," refuses to cooperate.
    b. tries too hard, is immobilized by perceived failure. _____

15. a. makes little or no effort to succeed, shows disdain for activities, voices anger or displeasure at parents, teachers, and students who offer assistance.
    b. verbalizes or expresses an attitude of apathy, shows no willingness to try. _____

Interpreting the Stress Reaction Scale for Reading

> *True opinions can prevail only if the facts to which they refer are known; if they are not known, false ideas are just as effective as true ones, if not a little more effective.*
>
> Walter Lippmann
> *Liberty and the News*

To determine the *fight* reactions, count the number of *a*'s circled. For the *flight* reactions, count the number of *b*'s. Typically, one pattern will dominate. It is not unusual for a student to have some *a*'s and some *b*'s circled or to have some *N/O*'s recorded. Even if one reaction is not dominant, the information still can be used to help design individualized intervention.

The Stress Reaction Scale for Reading is a useful supplement to other techniques used to measure reading. Reading assessment needs to be multidimensional and ongoing; it should not stop when initial assessment information is analyzed and intervention begun. The critical difference between using only the results of standardized and informal skills tests to design intervention and supplementing this information using data from the Stress Reaction Scale for Reading is it causes teachers to focus on the students' coping behavior during reading as much as on their skills deficits.

Adequate reading assessment

Adequate assessment should include observation, interviews, tests, and feedback.

Observation is used to determine the student's behavior toward learning or reading in specific situations and to assess competencies. The

Gentile and McMillan

teacher should observe the student in the classroom, particularly during reading and testing, and on the playground or in social situations with peers and adults.

Interviews with the student, parents, and other teachers are used to gather information related to the student's educational, social, and physical history; behavior; coping skills; interests; assets; abilities; and incentives for learning. The interview process also helps the teacher gain support from others for intervention.

Tests are designed to determine skills strengths and weaknesses. And, by using observational techniques, they can help identify behavior, coping styles, and reading expectancy levels. Both standardized tests and informal inventories should be used.

Feedback to the student, parents, and other school personnel is used to review results of assessment and suggest an intervention plan. Some examples of the kind of information teachers need to acquire during the assessment process include the following:

- Are there any organic or neurological problems that would preclude this student from reading at the expected level? (This will apply to a small percentage of students with reading difficulties.)
- At what level should this student be expected to read?
- How long will it take to achieve this level?
- At what level is the student currently reading?
- What are the student's specific strengths and weaknesses in reading?
- What does the student do when reading (or tests) becomes difficult?
- What coping skills does the student demonstrate in stressful situations?
- How often, and under what circumstances, do these behaviors interfere with performance? How, and under what circumstances, does this student cope successfully?
- Is there a dominant reaction pattern of fight or flight in stressful situations?
- What are the student's academic, social, artistic, or athletic strengths and interests?
- What are the student's favorite activities that can serve as incentives during intervention?
- What are reasonable and measureable short and long term goals for intervention with this student?
- What role can parents or other important persons play in the intervention process?

Teachers' self-assessment

An additional, vital element of the reading assessment frequently over-looked is the teacher's self-assessment. The teacher's mediation process, internal dialogue, and belief system are as critical to the success of the intervention as are those of the student. Teachers may be threatened by working with students demonstrating fight or flight reactions to reading for several reasons:

- In the absence of the required training or framework for working effectively with these students, teachers are vulnerable and often re-spond in fight or flight patterns themselves.
- Teachers are aware that students' failure to demonstrate measurable progress in reading may reflect on their professional evaluation.
- Using only skills based materials and instructional methods does not demonstrate the kind of change in students' reading that makes teachers feel competent or confident.
- Finally, teachers may dislike students because of their resistance or helplessness.

Teachers should be able to answer the following questions affirma-tively:

- Do I enjoy reading and do I read?
- Do I like teaching reading?
- Do I like my job?
- Do I believe this student can learn to read at the expected level?
- Do I believe I can help this student achieve that level?
- Do I want to work with this student?

A negative answer to even one of these questions can be a source of teacher stress that, if unresolved, may create barriers to successful inter-vention, no matter how well it is designed.

Helping students overcome their anxiety to become effective readers can be rewarding for teachers. But teachers need to identify and cope effec-tively with their own stress to avoid contributing to or perpetuating the anxiety experienced by students. Ultimately, the teacher must act as a reso-lute, enthusiastic model for these students to demonstrate the value of be-coming a reader, how to read, and, most importantly, the appropriate coping skills in stressful situations. This requires self-knowledge and self-control and also suggests a broader definition of teacher training.

3

Intervention

*...for a conscious being, to exist is to change, to change is to mature, to
mature is to go on creating oneself endlessly.*

Henri Bergson
Creative Evolution

When reading is stressful, students often try to avoid or escape the
source of their discomfort. Fight or flight reactions tend to reinforce themselves because they reduce a student's anxiety. Therefore, such
reactions are resistant to change.

After a student's pattern of responses to reading has been determined,
the next step is to plan appropriate intervention. When working with students who demonstrate a fight or flight response, it is important to understand the types of interactions that may take place between the student and
the teacher. As Figure 1 shows, students who are well adjusted readers tend
to have flexible, adaptive relationships with the teacher and approach reading willingly. The student who exhibits a fight response avoids reading by
confronting the teacher, thus leaving the assignment behind. The student
with a flight response escapes from both reading and the teacher.

A teacher working with a student who demonstrates a fight reaction to
reading must design a strategy that moves the student away from the con-
frontation and back to the reading assignment. This approach should be
concise and consistent, with a minimum of verbal interaction and prompting.

When the student flees the stressful tasks of reading, the teacher must
focus on drawing the student out and moving the student toward the task
and the teacher. This requires direct intervention, prompting, and talking.

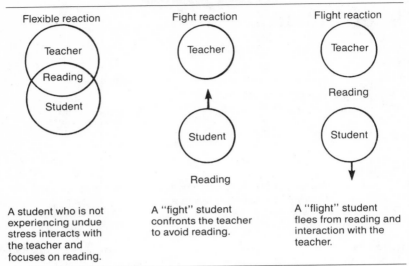

Figure 1
Stress reactions to reading

Flexible reaction

Teacher
Reading
Student

Fight reaction

Teacher
Student
Reading

Flight reaction

Teacher
Reading
Student

A student who is not experiencing undue stress interacts with the teacher and focuses on reading.

A "fight" student confronts the teacher to avoid reading.

A "flight" student flees from reading and interaction with the teacher.

With the "fight" student, the teacher must rechannel the confrontative behavior so the energy used to combat the teacher is applied to reading. This is often easier to achieve than successful intervention with the "flight" student. The fight reaction has a force behind it that, when redirected, is useful for overcoming reading difficulties. The flight reaction contains no such force. It is the absence of energy or motivation that makes working with the flight student so difficult. Figure 2 shows how these coping styles differ.

As Figure 2 indicates, attempts to remediate these students' reading difficulties must include not only skills development but also must emphasize acquiring the appropriate behavior to overcome reading difficulties and belief in their ability to master these problems. There is a difference between possessing reading skills and being able to apply them under challenging, difficult, or stressful circumstances. This requires students with reading difficulties to develop self-regulatory skills in order to cope. In the absence of these skills, most students resort to self-defeating behavior to expunge the threat reading poses to them, whether it be loss of self-esteem, frustration, or fear of ridicule. According to Manzo (1987):

Gentile and McMillan

Figure 2
Coping styles of students who perceive reading as threatening

	Fight	Flight
Student's internal dialogue	• "I won't read and you can't make me."	• "I can't read and no one can teach me."
Stress reactions	• Deprecates reading, books, teacher, and school	• Deprecates self
	• Confronts teacher to avoid reading	• Retreats into fantasy, silence, or daydreams, moving away from teacher and reading
	• Anxiety and energy directed outward	• Anxiety and energy turned inward
	• Yells or becomes hostile, obstinate, and resistive; acts out feelings by having tantrums, throwing objects, resisting	• Cries, pouts, or appears sad, despondent, or helpless; whines, quits easily
	• Moves past reading task to disrupt, deter, or distract the teacher	• Withdraws and does little to approach reading independently; tries to gain sympathy and help by "proving" inadequacies; requires constant supervision and guidance
Teacher's response	• Generally the teacher becomes involved in a power struggle with the student	• Generally the teacher tries to "rescue" the student

Whenever anyone is distressed it creates a preoccupation with the emotionally charged issue which in turn causes disruption of clear thinking, perception, and not surprisingly test like performance. "Common sense psychology" also suggests that when learning does not become generative, that is, beginning to roll along and grow between instructional periods, the child clearly is not thinking about, rehearsing, and applying what has been taught. Ultimately, all learning has to become self-determined or it simply will not occur in any profound way.

Students with reading difficulties must learn to deal directly with the stress they experience during reading by reappraising the threat and developing positive ways of coping with it. These stress reducing methods, called direct or self-regulating coping skills (Blackham & Silberman, 1980; Hilgard, Atkinson, & Atkinson, 1975), must be taught as diligently as functional reading skills because they help students master their reading difficulties and produce long term, positive effects during reading instruction.

Students whose responses to reading are fight or flight need to be taught three major self-regulatory skills: goal setting, self-incentives, and self-monitoring (Bandura, 1977; Kanfer, 1980; Runck, 1982).

Goal setting

If you can conceive it, you can achieve it.

Jesse Jackson

White (1959) posited that humans have a basic, lifelong drive for ordering and mastering the environment. This drive is so strong that, where order does not exist, a person will tend to impose order on external phenomena. Ordering the environment reduces uncertainty about what to expect, giving the individual better powers of prediction and control and, hence, reinforcing feelings of security by reducing the anxiety associated with uncertainty (Athey, 1985).

Teachers can help students regulate their reading difficulties by establishing explicit, reasonable, and reachable goals. Getting students to make self-directed changes in their reading requires the development of standards and goals to motivate and guide them. Bandura (1985, p.9) described this process:

> When people commit themselves to explicit goals, negative discrepancies between what they do and what they seek to achieve serve as motivators for change. By making self-satisfaction contingent on goal attainment, people persist in their efforts until their attainments match what they are seeking to achieve.

The purpose of many reading assignments may be unclear or meaningless to students with reading difficulties. These students do not understand that what they are doing will help them become better readers and improve their chances of succeeding in school. Reading assignments seem unrelated to their goals and provide no assistance in overcoming their educational or personal problems. In fact, these assignments may only highlight their perceived incompetencies. Teachers can aid students with reading difficulties by helping them establish explicit goals and by providing performance feedback.

Whether students with reading difficulties are motivated or discouraged when they fail to attain goals they have set for themselves is ultimately determined by their perceptions of their capacity to attain the goal. "Those who doubt their capabilities are easily discouraged by failure, whereas those who are highly assured of their efficacy for goal attainment intensify their efforts when their attainments fall short, and persevere until they succeed" (Bandura, 1985, p. 10).

Research has shown goal setting along with performance feedback to be highly effective in developing self-motivation (Locke et al., 1981). The degree to which establishing goals is an incentive for self-directed change in reading is dependent on three things:

1. *The explicitness of the goals.* Explicit goals provide clear guides for action as well as the means for students and teachers to evaluate performance. General goals are too vague and fail to direct students' motivation and behavior in reading instruction.

2. *The level of the goals.* Setting reasonable goals, working through incremental instructional steps, and making constructive appraisals of achievement sustain students' motivation and self-directed changes in reading. Students who set unrealistically high goals for improving their reading are disappointed when they fail to fulfill them.

3. *The proximity of the goals.* The effectiveness of goals is largely determined by how far into the future they are projected. Proximal goals mobilize effort and direct what one does now. By focusing on the future, it is too easy to temporize efforts at change in the present. "One can always begin in earnest in the tomorrows of each day" (Bandura, 1985, pp. 10-11). Students with reading difficulties must establish short term goals they can accomplish realistically. These subgoals can be the basis for greater achievement in the future. They also provide continuous incentives and guides for self-regulation that build a sense of competence, self-satisfaction and motivation. If students concentrate on improving their reading each day in class, in a year's time they will be well on the road to attaining their long term goals.

Self-incentives

The education of the will is the object of our existence.
Ralph Waldo Emerson
Society and Solitude

The second step in developing students' direct coping or self-regulating reading skills is to help them establish incentives to work and to provide themselves with tangible rewards when they reach established goals. Bandura (1985, p. 11) adds:

> People can get themselves to do things they would otherwise put off or avoid altogether by arranging incentives for subgoal attainments. They achieve greater self-directed change if they reward their successful efforts than if they provide no incentives for themselves. Evaluative self-incentives also serve as important self-motivators and guides for behavior. People get themselves to put forth the effort necessary to accomplish what they value for the satisfaction they derive from fulfilling the goals they set for themselves.

Students' incentives are highly individual. It is important that teachers take the time to define each student's incentives. While some incentives can be used effectively for groups of students, the most powerful and sustaining are those identified by students themselves. Ultimately, there is a big difference between developing an inner desire to be an effective reader and being extrinsically motivated to read by rewards or punishments from teachers, parents, or peers.

Self-monitoring

Most powerful is he who has himself in his own power.
Seneca the Younger
Epistolae Morales

As a final step in helping students acquire coping or self-regulatory skills, teachers must help them monitor the behavior they seek to change (Kazdin, 1974). Encouraging students to keep track of their stress level and the events that foster it during reading serves several purposes. Bandura (1985) points out that when students observe their own behavior and the circumstances under which it occurs, they can use their observations to identify what causes particular behaviors they may want to modify. Self-monitoring also provides necessary information for setting realistic sub-goals and for evaluating progress.

Sports provide a model for demonstrating the importance of self-monitoring. A weight lifter, for example, can record the increasing number of presses or curls and can see increased muscle structure. This positive feedback encourages continued effort and improvement (Horn, 1986). Teachers need to set up the same kind of circumstances for students during reading instruction.

Teachers or students can observe incremental gains in reading and provide feedback. To insure long term effects, students with reading difficulties must have reasons to change and the means to do so. Neither goals without performance feedback nor performance feedback without goals achieves any lasting change (Bandura and Cervone, 1984).

Before positive changes can occur, students must recognize their problems, acknowledge the nature of those problems, and gain control using adaptive stress reducing behaviors. This means sizing up the situation accurately and attempting to solve problems.

Entwisle (1971) suggested that "control beliefs" are especially important in reading because middleclass parents teach their children to expect order and meaning in their daily lives and to develop alternative strategies for dealing with problems that appear to violate this order. Other children's early education may be deficient in these respects. When children expect reading to be a system with its own internal meaning and consistency as well as a tool to help solve other problems, they are often excited about learning to read. If students do not see reading as having these characteristics, reading becomes "one more thing" imposed on unwilling victims by powerful authority figures (Athey, 1985).

The role of the teacher

> We should honor our teachers more than our parents, because while our parents cause us to live, our teachers cause us to live well.
>
> Philoxnus
> Quoted by Strobaeus, "Florilegium"

The teacher's role is crucial in creating an instructional environment that leads students to success. This is accomplished by modeling and by assisting students in developing attainable goals, providing consistent feedback, and eliciting self-evaluative information concerning reading performance. A structured, purposeful approach is vital to the process of self-regulation and remediation in reading.

Students with reading difficulties must learn to apply self-regulating skills steadily and consistently in attempting increasingly challenging and sometimes stressful assignments. Teachers must help students gain confidence in attempting more difficult reading tasks.

Immediate success is essential for students who have a history of difficulty or failure in reading. However, these students must gradually learn to struggle with adversity and to overcome their problems, even if they do encounter occasional failure.

Eventually students learn that their difficulty or failure in reading may be more attributable to a lack of effort than to a lack of ability or to external factors. Research on learned helplessness indicates that, with few exceptions, more reading difficulties result from students' lack of effort than from their lack of ability. Thus, the issue is not whether teachers can always prevent adversity or stress in reading, but how they can help students cope when it occurs.

Teachers need to work with students in the following three ways:

1. *Help students gain control over their reading responses.* Students need to identify their maladaptive stress reactions to reading and develop more strategies — such as goal setting, incentives, and self-monitoring — to deal with problems. Only then can they experience success as readers.

2. *Help students gain confidence and competence as readers.* Students need to be shown how to apply the necessary skills to complete reading assignments successfully. This means more than mastering isolated skills; it means developing the necessary self-control to study and process written information for purposes of taking tests, making oral and written reports, and contributing to class discussions.

3. *Help students gain closure and learn to cope successfully with their reading difficulties through self regulation.* This includes helping them overcome their fear or anger toward reading by identifying and reinforcing purposeful reading activities, mastering incremental learning steps, and establishing a schedule for accomplishing

Gentile and McMillan

the work. Students cannot alter what has happened to them in the past, but they can pursue solutions to current problems through prediction, flexibility, concentration, careful preparation, and practice.

Teachers can benefit from the concepts of "goodness of fit" and "poorness of fit" when working with students whose reading difficulties are compounded by their fight or flight stress responses. Goodness of fit occurs in reading when the instructional approach and teacher expectations are in concert with the student's capacities, motivations, and values. A good fit leads to success as measured by reading skills improvement and by observable, positive behavior changes. On the other hand, a poor fit involves discord between the student and the instructional approach and teachers' demands and expectations, so that distorted development and emotional maladjustment occur. This does not mean, however, that where there is a good fit there is an absence of pressure or stress. These are inescapable in the developmental reading process where new challenges, expectations, demands for change, and increasingly higher levels of achievement must be reached as the student advances through school.

Demands, stresses, and conflicts in reading are supportive and constructive when they are compatible with the student's developmental potential, capacities, motivations, personality, and values. But stress that occurs as the result of a poor fit between the instructional approach and the student's fight or flight responses may trigger emotional maladjustment and difficulty in reading.

Typically, students with reading difficulties develop a perception of reading and of themselves as readers that is geared to failure. They expect to do poorly and to fail; consequently they do both. Their apprehension makes them anxious enough to force these outcomes. Teachers are like good coaches. They must push students to do their best, sometimes beyond their abilities; help them overcome the fear of failure so they will take risks; and provide safety nets to catch them when they stumble. Teachers must also develop special relationships with these students, providing patience, understanding, and knowledge to help them overcome weaknesses or deficits and achieve group and individual goals.

Finally, it is important to consider what happens when the teacher is experiencing professional or personal stress (Deci et al., 1982). Students who exhibit fight or flight stress reactions may be particularly sensitive and vulnerable. Teachers must take care that their problems do not interfere with teaching or learning and accelerate what is already a stressful situation for these students.

Phillips Memorial
Library
Providence College

The role of the parent

You are the bows from which your children as living arrows are sent forth.

Kahlil Gibran
The Prophet

In many cases, early unrealistic expectations, inappropriate reactions, and inconsistencies in the family contribute to the development of a student's inappropriate coping behavior and stress reactions. Thus, the student, the teacher, and the parents must agree upon an intervention plan and goals.

Many students with reading difficulties experience high levels of stress in their homes and social lives. They often come from families where healthy psychological and academic development is inhibited. Some parents apply inordinate discipline when their children do not make satisfactory progress; others overprotect their children, often at great cost to themselves or other family members; others reject their youngsters' efforts in everything, forever anticipating failure (Gentile & McMillan, 1981).

A student's reading difficulty can create stress for parents, many of whom feel guilty. Parents may sense they have not given enough time or attention to their children and have failed to meet their needs. Parents who feel guilty sometimes become too preoccupied with their own emotional needs to help their youngsters adjust. Some parents become overly protective or smothering and compound their children's reading problems by protecting them from necessary challenges. Other parents feel resentful: "What did we do to deserve this?" Impatience, even rejection of a child, may result.

A youngster who is constantly rejected or ignored may react with anger, anxiety, or withdrawal. As the child becomes alienated from parents, teachers, siblings, or peers, the possibility of overcoming the reading difficulty is further reduced. In this situation, the threat reading poses for a child is as disabling as any skills deficit. Consequently, teachers must gain parents' cooperation and understanding to help these youngsters make adaptive rather than fight or flight responses to reading when it is stressful for them.

Gentile and McMillan

Summary

Students with reading difficulties must be taught to set explicit, reasonable goals for themselves, arrange rewards and incentives for their efforts, monitor and track their self-defeating reactions when reading is stressful, and use a variety of direct coping strategies instead of relying on a single ineffective technique. The roles of teachers and parents are significant in helping students make these behavioral adjustments. Teachers and parents must be cautious not to let their own emotional needs or reactions interfere with a youngster's ability to cope with reading when it is difficult.

4

Differentiated intervention: A plan for working with students

Self-reverence, self-knowledge, self-control. These three alone lead life to soverign power.

Alfred, 1st Lord Tennyson
Oenone

Many educational practices apply to all students, including those having problems with reading: firm, fair, consistent treatment that develops positive student/teacher relationships; support and encouragement; motivational techniques; interesting materials that provide opportunities for immediate success; incremental challenges and feedback; appropriate discipline; and a flexible, varied program (Harris, 1978; Spache, 1976).

Some specific factors also have been found useful for reducing anxiety in reading, including teaching relaxation techniques to students (Blake, 1984; Frey, 1980; Orlow, 1974; Zenker & Frey, 1985), proper nutrition (Chernick, 1980; Pertz & Putnam, 1982), and teaching study or test taking skills (Hoffman, 1983; Jacobs, 1966; Shilling, 1984; Simpson, 1984; Stewart & Green, 1983).

While all of these practices are helpful, teachers also benefit from a structured interventional plan for use with students who exhibit fight or flight behavior. We have been successful using the following general steps (adapted from Homme et al., 1969) for instructional intervention with groups or individual students who exhibit fight or flight responses to reading instruction.

1. The teacher and student agree on an accurate description of the problem.
2. The teacher and student clearly establish the need and purpose for change.

3. The teacher and student agree on a description of specific purposes and goals for reading.
4. The teacher and student establish a time frame for accomplishing purposes and goals for reading.
5. The teacher and student identify and define incentives for improving reading performance.
6. The teacher designs incremental instructional steps for learning that will permit the student to succeed in reading. The teacher should share this information with parents and show them how to support it. Putting the information in the form of a written contract is helpful with some students and parents.
7. The teacher provides the student and parents with consistent feedback on the student's reading skills acquisition and self-regulatory or coping skills.
8. The teacher sets the stage for further reading instructional sessions.

The structure of this plan is basically the same for working with both fight and flight students; it works with any reading instructional program. However, the content and the teacher's approach must vary according to each student's specific fight or flight response to reading. At the initial session, after the teacher, student, and parents have agreed on the interventional plan, it is important for the teacher to establish rules for working with the student. This is done by describing and agreeing on the teacher's responsibility, the student's responsibility, what the teacher is going to do and why, what the student is going to do and why, and what the consequences will be for the student when agreed upon goals and purposes are or are not reached.

A teacher who uses this structured interventional plan for changing students' inappropriate coping behavior is acting as a contingency manager. Blackham and Silberman (1980, p. 44) explain the advantages of contingency management:

> When a contingency manager says: "When you do A, then consequence B will follow," a promise or contract is operating between the two parties. When a person is informed that if he performs in a certain way he will escape or avoid an undesirable consequence, the stated contingency is a negative contingency contract. On the other hand, when an individual is informed that if he performs in a certain way he will acquire something he desires, a positive contingency contract is operating. The positive contingency contract is designed to influence the execution of a desired behavior. The negative contingency contract is intended to prevent the

occurrence of an undesirable behavior. Both types of contingency contracts may achieve the intended outcomes, but a positive contingency contract is preferable in most situations.

Contingency management is effective for changing students' behavior because reinforcing conditions take the form of events or activities. Blackham and Silberman continue: "Opportunities to perform desired activities are used to reinforce infrequently performed responses. In this sense, we can say that reinforcing responses (rather than reinforcing stimuli) increase the frequency or strength of the desirable responses. For example, when a person is permitted to engage in behavior B, the opportunity to perform behavior A reinforces behavior B. Behavior is maintained or changed as a result of its consequences; that is, behavior is a function of reinforcement."

The chance to do what one would like to do is a generally accepted motivational tool. A low probability behavior can be reinforced by the opportunity to engage in a high probability behavior (Premack, 1959). Many parents have used this principle successfully with such directives as "When you finish your homework, you may watch television."

Teachers acquire information from the complete assessment to help them use contingency management principles to intervene with avoidant reading responses. A detailed plan that covers one session follows. It provides specific examples of the varied approaches necessary to work to change students' fight or flight stress reactions to reading.

General approach to a one hour session with a fight or flight student

STEP 1. General approach

The teacher establishes rules and identifies:
- Teacher's responsibilities
- Student's responsibilities
- What teacher will do and how
- What student will do and how
- Consequences for student when goals for sessions are or are not reached

Variation for fight student

Limited verbal interaction; teacher consistent, clear, and direct. No extra discussion, teacher focuses on tasks. Student required to repeat rules and instructions.

Variation for flight student

Teacher and student discuss student's feelings objectively; teacher empathetic but avoids "sympathy trap." Teacher provides directions concerning student's perceived tendencies to quit, give up, appear helpless, or feign illness in order to avoid reading. Examples of these behaviors are presented from observing student during reading or testing.

STEP 2. General approach

The teacher describes the purposes and goals for reading and incremental instructional steps.
- "Our purposes for reading are...."
- "These are important because...."
- "You will have this much time to finish this much work."
- "When you are finished you can do such and such."

Student is asked to repeat:
- Purposes and goals for reading
- Why the purposes and goals are important
- How much time is given to complete the work
- Consequences when purposes and goals for session are or are not reached

Variation for fight student

The teacher explains to the student how resistant behavior during reading leads to difficulty and failure. It is made clear to the student that these reactions are self-defeating and must be changed. The teacher negotiates nothing with the student. The approach is one of barring all exits and trapping the student into reading and learning. The teacher's focus is on rechanneling the student's energy by "smuggling" reading instruction into a curriculum built on the youngster's interests and self-identified incentives. The message to the student is, "You can do this work, there is no alternative, and it's to your advantage to do it. When you finish *you* can do such and such."

Variation for flight student

The teacher explains that some of what the student is asked to do may be difficult, but the student will never be asked to do more than is possible. It is made clear that when the work becomes difficult the teacher will provide assistance but the student will be expected to try to overcome these difficulties and complete the assignment. The teacher's focus is on generating the student's willingness to try.

Gentile and McMillan

The amount of work and the time in which it is to be done are negotiable and can be adjusted. The message to the student is, "The surest way not to succeed is not to try. I will help you succeed. We are working together, but you are responsible to read and learn. When you finish, *we* will do such and such."

STEP 3. General approach

The teacher models the appropriate behavior for successfully completing the work. The focus is on responding effectively to difficult or stressful situations. A sample lesson is presented. Basic and special vocabulary from the lesson are introduced before the student is asked to read. The teacher makes sure the student is successful with the practice exercise. Criteria are defined for successful completion of each task.

Variation for fight student

The teacher confirms the student's ability to do the assigned work. Instructions are concise. The focus is on getting the student to work and on moving the teacher into the background. The teacher must be prepared for acting out behaviors, but must remain implacable and resolute when these occur. The fight student is often hypervigilant and prone to diversion, so opportunities for distraction must be reduced as much as possible.

Variation for flight student

The teacher models the appropriate behavior for overcoming the student's anxiety during reading (relaxation training, positive imagery, test taking skills), furnishes expanded instructions, and provides a "safety net" by being available for direct assistance should the student encounter problems during the work. The student is encouraged to take some risks and work independently. Activities are designed to assure success and, gradually, to provide opportunity to work apart from the teacher for varied periods.

STEP 4. General approach

Reading lessons are developed to build word recognition, vocabulary, comprehension, and study or test taking skills. They may include silent or oral activities and should require 10 to 12 minutes to complete. The time may be shorter or longer depending on the task and the student. These exercises should be constructed according to the student's interests, but should be congruent with regular classroom or content area reading requirements (Allington & Shake,

1986). The teacher reinforces appropriate reading and coping skills, provides additional instructions, and restates rules whenever necessary.

Variation for fight student

The teacher sets up the lesson and gets the student working as soon as possible. Should the student encounter difficulty, the teacher acts as a resource, but help is provided in an objective, matter of fact way. The teacher's focus remains on the tasks and expectations. The level of performance and the time for completing the work are consistently and firmly established.

Variation for flight student

The teacher makes it clear that the student will have help when it is needed and assures success by starting with a sample lesson. The teacher makes sure the student is successful with this activity before proceeding. The teacher acts as an emotional support when the student encounters difficulty, but always insists on the student trying. The student is never given too much to do in too short a time. What the teacher assigns must be completed, but standards for evaluating the outcomes should be flexible.

STEP 5. General approach

Feedback and closure. The teacher evaluates the student's performance and makes sure strengths as well as weaknesses are discussed. Inappropriate coping behaviors are identified, and the teacher models appropriate behaviors. Progress is recorded, and the student is given clear indication of mastery or achievement. This information is shared with parents and other teachers.

Variation for fight student

Occasionally, the teacher asks the student to discuss reactions to reading and describe inappropriate and appropriate behavior. The student is asked to role play an appropriate coping skill that helped complete one portion of the assignment. This is helpful because some fight students are perfectionists. They frequently are good at other things, such as sports, music, or art. This approach shows the student how to control the situation in reading in order to succeed. The teacher occasionally asks the student to become the teacher. Role reversal helps strengthen the effects of the teacher's modeling and provides a basis for building trust with the fight student in reading.

Variation for flight student

The teacher assumes the role of coach and encourages the student to continue working to develop appropriate reading and coping skills, pointing out details of improved performance in reading. The teacher also encourages the student to demonstrate a skill apart from reading in order to gain confidence in the ability to perform and to build a trusting relationship with the flight student.

STEP 6. General approach

Setting the stage for further learning. The teacher reviews samples of the previous lesson and confirms the student's understanding or knowledge. Portions of the lesson the student cannot recall are reviewed. Then, the teacher proceeds to the next incremental step with new material. Most of these students require guidelines and previews of "coming attractions." The teacher furnishes a clear picture of the next lesson, models the new activity, and sets time limits for completing it. If there is any need for these students to prepare homework, the teacher explains the assignment, then asks, "What are you going to have to do to be ready for tomorrow's work?" The student must restate:

- How to prepare the material
- Why it is important
- When homework will be done
- What will be brought back to class and the consequences for returning or not returning material
- How material will be evalutated

Variation for fight student

In the event that the student does not finish what is assigned during a particular lesson, the material should be completed as homework and brought to the next session. How much or what should be done is negotiable. The teacher makes it clear that the student is responsible and accountable for the work being finished. Developing a contract with the student in these circumstances can add leverage to the teacher's position. When the work is done to the teacher's satisfaction, the student is reinforced.

Variation for flight student

The teacher uses prompting and encouragement to guide the student to the next lesson. Time is made available to complete portions of the previous day's work whenever it is appropriate. The teacher makes a point of showing the student evidence of improved performance in reading. Equal emphasis is placed on the student's attempts to use more effective coping skills and on identifying reading skills development. A limited amount of homework may encourage the student to take some risks while working independently.

STEP 7. General approach

To maintain successful intervention, the teacher should:

- Observe the student and encourage appropriate coping behaviors, but not reward inappropriate responses.
- Establish a tempo that keeps the student engaged and on task.
- Establish a relationship with the student based on trust.
- Make sure each reading assignment has a concrete progress check to determine sufficient mastery or achievement.
- Gear instruction to meaningful work, "catch the student doing things right," and provide appropriate reinforcement.
- Discuss the student's self-talk and the role it plays in developing inappropriate or appropriate coping skills in reading; help the student identify phrases that can alleviate anxiety and provide encouragement.

Variation for fight student

The teacher must always have backup material ready to use with the fight student. Being able to shift gears is important when working with this student. In this way, the teacher can adjust the kind of work, level of difficulty or interest, and expectation. The focus should be on maintaining the student's time on task behavior, making a smooth transition from one activity to the next, and acknowledging the student's frustration from time to time, but allowing no shortcuts or escape from assignments. The teacher gets to know the student through the work. The emphasis is always on the task. The student's energy against the teacher and reading must be redirected to the assignment. The teacher establishes a time frame for completing the work. Consequences for inappropriate behavior or performance are clearly described and executed. Reinforcement is provided as reading and coping skills improve.

Variation for flight student

The teacher provides a flexible time schedule for the flight student. When the student does not complete all of an assignment, the teacher provides additional time. The student is encouraged to continue working and is ultimately reinforced upon completing the work. Afterwards, the teacher discusses the student's performance and praises the effort to employ appropriate coping skills to overcome stressful situations. The teacher gets to know the student through these personal discussions. This is an important distinction, because the student tends to retreat into silence or fantasy when reading becomes difficult and a considerable amount of energy is turned against the self. The student can be "brought out" by moving him or her toward the teacher, then to the work. Incentives are identified for working to capacity. Reinforcement is furnished as the student demonstrates appropriate reading and coping skills.

Summary

If students who respond to reading with fight or flight behavior are identified early, they can be helped to change their perception of reading as threatening or stressful and to develop more appropriate, successful ways to cope with the stress they experience in reading. These students also can be expected to progress as readers without continual remedial instruction. However, it appears that a growing number of these students are enrolled in ongoing remedial programs (Gentile & McMillan, 1984; Lamb, 1985; Swain, 1985). This is a difficult situation to change because students who have developed flight coping patterns in reading are often "rescued" by well meaning parents, teachers, or school administrators and are socially promoted. On the other hand, those students who fight teachers and reading are frequently referred out of regular classrooms to receive special help. Neither the rescuing nor the special help directly addresses these students' central problem, the avoidance of reading and learning. Consequently, little happens to change students' inappropriate coping behavior so they can learn effective ways of managing stress.

Furthermore, remedial work in reading typically does not keep pace with teachers' expectations in the regular classroom or equip students to return to class and work at grade level (Allington & Shake, 1986). Many students identified as having reading difficulties start down a remedial track from which they rarely escape. What begins as avoidance of a threatening task becomes a self-fulfilling prophecy. Too often a student with an unresolved fight or flight response ends up as a student who can read with minimal competency, but who never reads unless forced to do so.

Teachers must deal directly with the perception of reading as a threat and teach in a way that recognizes and responds to this problem. In this way, a more productive, less stressful learning environment can be created for the benefit of both learners and teachers.

A final word: Prevention

The summer I was four years old my mother bought me my first book and started teaching me to read. One night at bedtime...my father wanted to see how I was progressing with the written word.

They placed me between them with the opened book. I knew a few words, but under pressure to perform forgot everything....I didn't recognize a word.

My father saved my pride....Taking the book in hand, he moved me close against him and rubbed his cheek against mine. "Now," he said, pointing to a word, "you know that word don't you?" I did indeed. " 'The,' " I said. "You're a smart boy. I bet you know this one too." " 'Boy,' " I said....

That night they let me sleep between them.

Russell Baker
Growing Up
(Congdon and Weed, 1982)

Ideally, no student would perceive reading as threatening. All students would have consistent, positive early reading experiences without anxiety, ridicule, fear of failure, or unrealistic expectations. Every student would arrive for the first day of school with enthusiasm for reading. Students and their parents would have confidence in students' ability to learn to read in a reasonable period of time.

Unfortunately, the opposite is true for many students. For some youngsters, anxiety over learning to read is compounded by some teachers' anxiety over being able to teach them to read. Teachers must be trained to provide students with challenging but less threatening reading instruction and to help students cope successfully when reading becomes difficult or stressful. McGinnis (1986, p. 22) said, "It is time that the research on learning to read and on acquiring self-control be brought into the mainstream and taught in teachers' colleges." Teachers working to help students overcome reading difficulties need to teach self-regulating skills as well as skills needed to decode and interpret print. Effective intervention can provide the basis for students reaching reading independence through self-correction and guidance. Overcoming fight or flight reactions to reading and sticking with the commitment that requires ultimately bring students desirable, long lasting rewards—a sense of self-discipline, self-esteem, and self-satisfaction—transferable to the world of work and other areas of life.

Stress and reading difficulties: For further learning

Those parents or teachers who would like to learn more about helping students make adaptive responses to fight or flight stress reactions can benefit from the following related readings.

Albert, L. *Coping with kids and school.* New York: Ballantine Books, 1984.

Anderson, E., Redman, G., and Rogers, C. *Self-esteem for tots to teens.* New York: Meadowbrook, 1984.

Bodenhamber, G. *Back in control.* Englewood Cliffs, NJ: Prentice-Hall, 1983.

Briggs, D.C. *Your child's self-esteem.* New York: Doubleday, 1970.

Clabby, J.F., and Elias, M. *Teach your child decision making.* Garden City, NY: Doubleday, 1986.

Dreikurs, R., and Soltz, V. *Children: The challenge.* New York: Hawthorne Books, 1964.

Dreikurs, R., and Grey, L. *A new approach to discipline: Logical consequences.* New York: Hawthorne Books, 1968.

Dreikurs, R., Grunwald, B.B., and Pepper, F.C. *Maintaining sanity in the classroom: Illustrated teaching techniques.* New York: Harper & Row, 1971.

Elkind, D. *The hurried child.* Reading, MA: Addison-Wesley, 1981.

Elkind, D. *All grown up and no place to go.* Reading, MA: Addison-Wesley, 1984.

Ginott, H.C. *Teacher & child.* New York: Avon Books, 1972.

Mitchell, W., and Conn, C.P. *The power of positive students.* New York: William Morrow, 1985.

Runyan, B., and Monson, S.W. *401 ways to get your kids to work at home.* New York: St. Martin's Press, 1981.

Smith, M.J. *Yes I can say no.* New York: Arbor House, 1986.

Youngs, B.B. *Stress in children.* New York: Arbor House, 1985.

Youngs, B.B. *Helping your teenager deal with stress.* Los Angeles: Jeremy P. Tarcher Inc., 1986.

References

Abrams, J. A critique of E. Gann's study: Reading difficulty and personality organization. In L.M. Gentile and M.L. Kamil (Eds.), *Reading research revisited.* Columbus, OH: Charles E. Merrill, 1983.

Allington, R.L. Poor readers don't get to read much in reading groups. *Language Arts,* 1980, *57* (8), 872-876.

Allington, R.L., and Shake, M.C. Remedial reading: Achieving curricular congruence in classroom and clinic. *The Reading Teacher,* 1986, *39* (7), 648-654.

Athey, I. Reading research in the affective domain. In H. Singer and R.B. Ruddell (Eds.) *Theoretical models and processes of reading,* third edition. Newark, DE: International Reading Association, 1985.

Bandura, A. *Social learning theory.* Paper presented at the Carnegie Conference on Unhealthful Risk-Taking Behavior in Adolescence, San Francisco, January 1985.

Bandura, A. *Social learning theory.* Englewood Cliffs, NJ: Prentice-Hall, 1977.

Bandura, A., and Cervone, D. *Differential engagement of self-reactive influences in motivation.* Unpublished manuscript, Stanford University, 1984.

Bird, G. Personality factors in learning. *The Personnel Journal,* 1927, *6,* 56-59.

Blackham, G.J., and Silberman, A. *Modification of child and adolescent behavior.* Belmont, CA: Wadsworth Publishing, 1980.

Blake, M.E. Reading in Denmark: A relaxed atmosphere is the key. *The Reading Teacher,* 1984, *38* (1), 42-47.

Blanchard, P. Reading disablties in relation to difficulties of personality and emotional development. *Mental Hygiene,* 1936, *20,* 384-413.

Cannon, W.B. *Bodily changes in pain, hunger, fear and rage.* New York: Appleton-Century, 1915.

Chernick, E. Effects of the Feingold diet on reading achievment and classroom behavior. *The Reading Teacher,* 1980, *34 (2),* 171-174.

Dahlberg, C.C., Roswell, F., and Chall, J. Psychotherapeutic principles as applied to remedial reading. *Elementary School Journal,* 1952, *53,* 211-217.

Deci, E.L. The well-tempered classroom—how not to motivate teachers and students: Impose stricter standards, more controls, and greater conformity. *Psychology Today,* March 1985, 52-53.

Deci, E.L., Spiegel, N.H., Ryan, R.M., Foestner, R., and Kaufman, M. Effects of performance standards on teaching styles: Behavior of controlling teachers. *Journal of Educational Psychology,* 1982, *74* (6), 852-859.

deHirsch, K., Jansky J.J., and Langford, W.S. *Predicting reading failure: A preliminary study.* New York: Harper & Row, 1966.

Dolch, E.W. *The psychology and teaching of reading.* Boston: Ginn, 1931.

Dolch, E.W. *The psychology and teaching of reading,* second edition. Champaign, IL: Garrard Press, 1951.

Dreikurs, R. Emotional predispositions to reading difficulties. *Archives of Pediatrics,* 1954, *71,* 340.

Dreikurs, R., Grunwald, B.B., and Pepper, F.C. *Maintaining sanity in the classroom: Illustrated teaching techniques.* New York: Harper & Row, 1971.

Dreikurs, R., and Soltz, V. *Children: The challenge.* New York: Hawthorn Books, 1964.

Elkind, D. *The hurried child: Growing up too fast too soon.* Reading, MA: Addison-Wesley, 1981.

Entwisle, D.R. Implications of language socialization for reading models and for learning to read. *Reading Research Quarterly,* 1971, *7* (1), 111-167.

Freud, A. Psychoanalysis and the training of the young child. *Psychiatric Quarterly,* 1935, *4,* 15-24.

Freud, A. *The ego and mechanisms of defense.* London: Hogarth, 1937.

Frey, H. Improving the performance of poor readers through autogenic relaxation training. *The Reading Teacher,* 1980, *33* (8), 928-932.

Gann, E. *Reading difficulty and personality organization.* New York: Kings Crown Press, 1945.

Gates, A.I. The role of personality maladjustment in reading disability. *Journal of Genetic Psychology,* 1941, *69,* 77-83.

Gentile, L.M., and Lamb, P. *A study of children's developmental reading expectancy levels: Some implications for classroom instruction.* Paper presented at the American Reading Forum National Conference, Orlando, Florida, December 1984.

Gentile, L.M., and McMillan, M.M. A commentary on Abrams' critique of Gann's study. In L.M. Gentile, M.L. Kamil, and J.S. Blanchard (Eds.), *Reading research revisited.* Columbus, OH: Charles Merrill, 1983, 484.

Gentile, L.M., and McMillan, M.M. Profiling problem readers: Diagnosis and prescription. *Academic Therapy,* 1981, *17* (1), 47-56.

Gentile, L.M., and McMillan, M.M. Stress as a factor in reading difficulties: From research to practice. Paper presented at the American Reading Forum National Conference, Orlando, Florida, December 1984.

Gentile, L.M., McMillan, M.M., and Swain, C. Parents' identification of children's life crises: Stress as a factor in reading difficulties. In G.H. McNinch (Ed.), *Reading research in 1984: Comprehension, computers, communication.* Fifth Yearbook of the American Reading Forum. Carrollton, GA: Thomasson Printing and Office Equipment, 1985.

Gray, W.S. *Remedial cases in reading: Their diagnosis and treatment.* Supplementary Educational Monographs No. 22. Chicago: University of Chicago Press, 1922.

Gray, W.S. *Summary of investigations relating to reading.* Supplementary Educational Monographs No. 28. Chicago: University of Chicago Press, 1925.

Harris, A.J. Practical suggestions for remedial teachers. *The Reading Teacher,* 1978, *31* (8), 916-922.

Hilgard, E.R., Atkinson, R.C., and Atkinson, R.L. *Introduction to psychology.* New York: Harcourt Brace Jovanovich, 1975.

Hincks, E.M. *Disability in reading and its relation to personality.* Harvard Monographs in Education No. 7. Cambridge: Harvard University Press, 1925.

Hoffman, S. Using student journals to teach study skills. *Journal of Reading,* 1983, *26* (4), 344-347.

Homme, L., Csanyi, A.P., Gonzales, M.A., and Rechs, J.R. *How to use contingency contracting in the classroom.* Champaign, IL: Research Press, 1969.

Horn, J.C. Pumping iron, pumping ego. *Psychology Today,* 1986, *20,* 16.

Huey, E.B. *The psychology and pedagogy of reading.* New York: Macmillan, 1908.

Jackson, J. A survey of psychological, social, and environmental differences between advanced and retarded readers. *The Journal of Genetic Psychology,* 1944, *65,* 113-131.

Jacobs, P.I. Effects of coaching on the College Board English Composition Test. *Educational and Psychological Measurement,* 1966, *26,* 55-67.

Johnson, P.H. Understanding reading disability. *Harvard Educational Review,* 1985, *55,* 153-177.

Kagan, J. Stress and coping in early development. In N. Garmezy and M. Rutter (Eds.), *Stress, coping, and development in children.* New York: McGraw-Hill, 1983.

Kagan, J., and Havemann, E. *Psychology: An introduction,* second edition. New York: Harcourt Brace Jovanovich, 1972.

Kanfer, F.H. Self-management methods. In F.H. Kanfer and P. Goldstein (Eds.), *Helping people change: A textbook of methods.* New York: Pergamon Press, 1980.

Kazdin, A.E. Self-monitoring and behavior change. In M.J. Mahoney and C.E. Thoresen (Eds.), *Self-control: Power to the person.* Monterey, CA: Brooks/Cole Publishers, 1974.

Kelly, J.B., and Wallerstein, J.S. The effects of parental divorce: Experiences of the child in early latency. *American Journal of Orthopsychiatry,* 1976, *46* (1), 20-32.

Lamb, P. *The symptoms of childhood depression as factors in children's reading difficulties.* Unpublished doctoral dissertation, North Texas State University, 1985.

Laurita, R.E. Child's reading ability linked to development of visual perception. *Educational Week,* 1985, *5* (7), 18.

Lecky, P. *Self-consistency: A theory of personality.* New York: Island Press, 1951.

Lloyd-Kolkin, D. *The California Staying Well News,* 1986, *2* (4), 1.

Locke, E.A., Shaw, K.N., Saari, L.M., and Latham, G.P. Goal setting and task performance: 1969-1980. *Psychological Bulletin,* 1981, *90,* 125-152.

Lynch, J.J., Long, J.M., Thomas, S.A., Malinow, K.L., and Katcher, A.H. The effects of talking on the blood pressure of hypertensive and normotensive individuals. *Psychosomatic Medicine,* 1981, *43* (1), 25-33.

Manzo, A.V. Psychologically induced dyslexia and learning disabilities. *The Reading Teacher,* 1987, *40*(4), 408-413.

Maxwell, M. The role of attitudes and emotions in changing reading and study skills behavior of college students. *Journal of Reading,* 1971, *14* (6), 359-364, 420-422.

McDermott, R.P. Social relations as contexts for learning. *Harvard Educational Review,* 1977, *47,* 198-213.

McGuinness, D. Facing the learning disabilities crisis. *Education Week,* 1986, *5,* 22-28.

Mehan, H. *Learning lessons.* Cambridge, MA: Harvard University Press, 1979.

Missildine, W.H. The emotional background of thirty children with reading difficulties. *The Nervous Child,* 1946, *5,* 263-272.

Moffett, J. Hidden impediments to improving English teaching. *Phi Delta Kappan,* 1985, *67,* 50-56.

Monroe, M. *Children who cannot read.* Chicago: University of Chicago Press, 1932.

Natchez, G. (Ed.). *Children with reading problems.* New York: Basic Books, 1968.

Natchez, G. *Personality patterns and oral reading: A study of overt behavior in the reading situation as it reveals reactions of dependence, aggression, and withdrawal in children.* New York: New York University Press, 1959.

Orlow, M. Low tolerance for frustration. *The Reading Teacher,* 1974, *27* (7), 667-674.

Osborn, W.J. Emotional blocks in reading. *Elementary School Journal,* 1951, *52,* 26.

Paynter, R.H., and Blanchard, P. *Study of educational achievement of problem children.* New York: The Commonwealth Fund, 1929.

Pertz, D.L., and Putnam, L.R. An examination of the relationship between nutrition and learning. *The Reading Teacher,* 1982, *35* (6), 702-706.

Premack, D. Toward empirical behavior laws: Positive reinforcement. *Psychological Review,* 1959, *66,* 219-233.

Preston, M. Reading failure and the child's security. *American Journal of Orthopsychiatry,* 1940, *10,* 252.

Robinson, H.A. Treatment of severe cases of reading disability. *Journal of Educational Research,* 1939, *32,* 531-535.

Robinson, H.A. (Ed). *Meeting individual differences in reading.* Proceedings of the Annual Conference on Reading held at the University of Chicago. Chicago: University of Chicago Press, 1964.

Robinson, H.A. *Why pupils fail in reading.* Chicago: University of Chicago Press, 1946.

Roswell, F.G., and Natchez, G. *Reading disability: A human approach to learning,* third edition. New York: Basic Books, 1977.

Rotter, J.G. Generalized expectancies for internal versus external control of reinforcement. *Psychological Monographs,* 1966, *80* (1).

Runck, B. *Behavioral self-control: Issues in treatment assessment.* Rockville, MD: National Institute of Mental Health Science Reports, 1982.

Rutter, M. Stress, coping, and development: Some issues and some questions. In N. Garmezy and M. Rutter (Eds.), *Stress, coping, and development in children.* New York: McGraw-Hill, 1983.

Selye, H. *The stress of life.* New York: McGraw-Hill, 1956.

Selye, H. *The stress of life,* revised edition. New York, McGraw-Hill, 1976.

Sherman, M. Emotional disturbances and reading disability. In W.S. Gray (Ed.), *Recent trends in reading.* Supplementary Educational Monographs No. 49. Chicago: University of Chicago Press, 1939.

Shilling, F.C. Teaching study skills in the intermediate grades—we can do more. *Journal of Reading,* 1984, *27* (7), 620-623.

Simpson, J.S. The status of study strategy instruction: Implications for classroom teachers. *Journal of Reading,* 1984, *28* (2), 136-142.

Skinner, B.F. Some issues concerning the control of human behavior. In *Cumulative record: A selection of papers.* New York: Meredith Corporation, 1972.

Spache, G.D. *Investigating the issues of reading disabilities.* Boston: Allyn & Bacon, 1976.

Stewart, O., and Green, D.S. Test-taking skills for standardized tests of reading. *The Reading Teacher,* 1983, *36* (7), 634-638.

Swain, C. *Stress as a factor in primary schoolchildren's reading difficulties.* Unpublished doctoral dissertation, North Texas State University at Denton, 1985.

Weinberg, W., and Rehmet, A. Childhood affective disorder and school problems. In D.F. Cantwell and G.A. Carlson (Eds.), *Affective disorders in childhood and adolescence: An update.* Englewood Cliffs, NJ: Spectrum Publications, 1983.

White, R.W. Motivation reconsidered: The concept of competence. *Psychological Review,* 1959, *66,* 297-333.

Wilson, R.M. *Diagnostic and remedial reading for classroom and clinic,* fourth edition. Columbus, OH: Charles E. Merrill, 1981.

Wiskell, W. The relationship between reading difficulties and psychological adjustment. *Journal of Educational Research,* 1948, *4* (7), 557-559.

Young, N., and Gaier, E.L. Implications in emotionally caused reading retardation. *Elementary English,* 1951, *28* (5), 271-275.

Zenker, E.R., and Frey, D.Z. Relaxation helps less capable students. *Journal of Reading,* 1985, *28* (4), 342-344.